How To Not Be A Racist

Practical Strategies on How To Stop Being Racist

John Anna

Table of Contents

Chapter 1

The History of Racism

Images of crowds gathered around fallen, spray-painted statues will surely rank among the most iconic pictures taken in 2020. The nation's attention has been drawn by the indictment of these monuments to the long-lasting legacy of slavery in the United States, which extends from the Middle Passage and Jim Crow laws to the long history of police brutality against African Americans, which served as the impetus for the Black Lives Matter movement in the first place.

There has never been a more important time to study American history related to racism and slavery. It is also impossible to comprehend how Europeans and their colonial "descendants" in the United States engineered the most thorough and persistent dehumanization of a people in history without an understanding of the relatively little-studied history of race as a concept.

The logic underlying the history of race initially appears to be deceptively clear: between the 15th and 18th centuries, Europeans and their American heirs felt it was necessary to degrade and revile their captives in order to justify the forced deportation of 400,000 Black Africans to North America and an additional eleven million to other parts of the Americas. However, racism as it exists today is not just a cancerous fallout from the American plantation system of the 19th century; it also originated from a complex and purportedly "scientific" European understanding of the human species that dates back to the Enlightenment.

Natural philosophers and savants on the Continent stopped turning to the Bible in the early eighteenth century to understand the origins of the human species. Naturalists used more "empirical" approaches to address one of the most important "anthropological" questions of the day: why did

Africans, millions of whom were already working on European plantations, look different from white Europeans? Their goal was to find physical explanations for natural phenomena.

There were a dozen or more supposedly scientific explanations available by the 17th century. Some said that black skin was caused by vapors that came from the skin; others said that darkened sperm or the power of the mother's imagination caused black skin to be passed down from generation to generation; still, others said that the heat or the air from the Torrid Zone darkened the humors and caused skin discoloration.

Degeneration, the dominant "anthropological" concept that arose around 1750, can be understood as the exact opposite of what we now know to be true about the origins of humankind. The degeneration theory contends that a superior white race once traveled around the world and underwent climatic mutations, in contrast to the model that explains how evolution and subsequent human migrations from the African continent account for humanity's diversity of colors. These morphological and pigmentation changes were explained as a perversion or deterioration of a higher archetype rather than as adaptations or products of natural selection.

Medical professionals intervened to clarify that imprecise story and lay the groundwork for the concept of what we now refer to as race. Specifically, anatomists dissected the bodies of allegedly degenerate Africans and wrote several shocking articles about the alleged harm caused by living in a tropical climate, including the existence of black sperm, black brains, black bile, and even racialized black lice.

The most racist European doctors blamed Black Africans for specific organ-based diseases, such as reduced intelligence and lethargy. Unsurprisingly, the propagation of these myths and the techniques used to create them took off in the US when Samuel A. Cartwright discovered two "diseases" linked to African Americans in 1851. First, there was a mental disorder known as drapetomania that made slaves flee. The second was dysaesthesia aethiopica, a kind of lethargy that affected

Africans who were neither under the control of white people nor kept as slaves. His remedy was to put a leather strap on them and anoint them with oil.

Additionally, Europe gave Americans the very concept of "race." Emmanuel Kant and J.F. Blumenbach, two prominent Germans by the 1770s—the latter creating the term "Caucasian" because he thought the original prototype race originated in the Caucus Region—affirmed that recent advances in biometrics and anatomy warranted the use of the modernistic term "race" to distinguish between different subspecies of humans.

Classification schemes based on race offered the most potent structure for comprehending the differences between White and Black people. Going one step further, some naturalists suggested that Africans belonged to a completely distinct species. This latter view was, predictably, embraced by some in the American pro-slavery lobby.

Beginning in the 1770s, progressive intellectuals, abolitionists, and eventually freed slaves such as author Olaudah Equiano, analyzed the causes and consequences of racial prejudice. However, despite the fact that scientific studies have demonstrated how incorrect Enlightenment theories of race were, many of the most antiquated and unscientific ideas about race from Europe have persisted to this day in the American psyche and are even a staple of the Alt-Right. In fact, the Trump Administration's immigration policies—which maintain that immigrants from some nations are more desirable than those from others—are essentially bringing back antiquated ideas about the supposedly deterministic nature of race.

It is imperative to consistently reject racialized thought, particularly when it is employed as a weapon by our politicians. Extending our understanding of racism to include the anecdotal, spurious, and pseudoscientific birth of these ideas centuries ago may contribute to an effective rebuttal to such malicious positions. In the end, all Americans may agree on this: regardless of our origins, we are all the unfortunate inheritors of a fatal and illegal science.

Additionally, from the sixteenth to the beginning of the nineteenth century, an era that is now known as Old Imperialism was dominant. Politicians needed to link empire building to a country's greatness, and social and religious factors bolstered the idea that Western civilization was superior to "backward" societies.

Europe gained dominance over Africa and Asia through annexation, economic spheres of influence, and direct military force. The adage "the sun never sets on the British Empire" aptly summed up Great Britain's position as the colonial powerhouse with the most colonies by 1914. The world at large, as well as the colonial countries, were impacted by imperialism. In addition, it sparked rivalry among countries and wars that would upend international harmony in 1914. Racism has developed through the larger "them" is defined by the very human inclination to identify with an "us." The legacy of American slavery is one of the causes of racism.

American slavery with the understanding that it started a century later, not in 1619, when the American colonies did. The most overt act of racism in world history is slavery, whose implementation has had lingering effects for over 500 years. Additionally, Racism has its roots in the mission to Christianize, in the differences between religions, and in the widespread acceptance of owning people who practice different faiths. It was acceptable for African people to own slaves from rival tribes, for Muslims to own slaves from other religions, and for Christians to own slaves from other religions.

To elaborate on the previous source, eugenics was one of the ways that Slavers used to defend their exploitation of Black people. This literally translates to "good birth," and it is evident in the notion that one race is superior to another, particularly in Aryarism. Anti-Semitism and animosity towards Jews are additional factors.

Notable political figures who have experienced racism include Dr. Martin Luther King Jr., whose dream was to end racial discrimination, Medgar Evers, who opposed violence, Thurgood Marshall, who was denied entry to universities, and Rosa Parks, who was detained for breaking state laws prohibiting segregation. Many leaders, including Dr. B.R. Ambedkar and Mahatma Gandhi, have experienced racial discrimination.

The British PM is currently dealing with racism-related issues. When the UK's Chancellor of the Exchequer plunged the country into economic chaos. Cleaning up the mess is now the responsibility of the Rishi Sunak. As he had forewarned during the competition, the rishi sunak was referred to as the "prescient." According to Pat Shipman's book, "The Evolution of Racism," racism is an outdated and repulsive mindset.

Racism is a challenge not just a challenge from politics, but also every single citizen's civic life. According to research, the majority of young Black British people have encountered racism at school, and two out of every three believe that racial stereotypes impede their ability to succeed academically. The predictability of this racism was one of its worst aspects. Light is the only force that can chase out darkness. Only love has the power to drive out hate. How long should we wait for the light and love to embrace is the question.

Chapter 2

Understanding Implicit Bias

Unconscious affiliation, attitude, or belief toward any social group is known as implicit bias. Stereotyping, the practice of attributing specific traits or characteristics to every member of a given group, is frequently caused by implicit biases. It's critical to keep in mind that implicit biases function almost exclusively at the unconscious level. Compared to explicit biases and prejudices, implicit biases are less deliberate and manageable.

Even if someone openly expresses disapproval of a particular attitude or belief, they may nevertheless be harboring unconscious biases of the same kind. These prejudices don't always fit with how we see ourselves or who we are. Additionally, people's associations with their own race, gender, sexual orientation, religion, and other personal traits can be either positive or negative.

Even though some people would prefer to think of themselves as immune to these implicit prejudices and stereotypes, the truth is that everyone uses them, whether they like it or not. However, this fact does not imply that you are inherently biased or predisposed to treat others unfairly. All it indicates is that associations and generalizations are being made by your brain while it is functioning.

It is typically impossible to isolate oneself from the influence of society, in addition to the fact that we are influenced by the stereotypes that already exist in the society into which we were born and our surroundings. Nonetheless, you can raise your awareness of how society affects you and how you unconsciously think.

These implicit biases develop as a result of the brain's innate propensity to filter, arrange, and classify information about the outside world. These inclinations make us vulnerable to bias:

We have a propensity to look for patterns: The brain's innate inclination to search for connections and patterns in the environment leads to implicit bias. This capacity to create associations about the outside world is an essential component of social cognition, which is our capacity to store, process, and apply information about individuals in social settings.

We prefer to take shortcuts: Implicit bias, like other cognitive biases, stems from the brain's inclination to simplify the world. Mental shortcuts help the brain process information faster and more easily because it is constantly exposed to more data than it could possibly process.

Social conditioning and our experiences both have an impact on implicit biases, which are attitudes that are shaped by experiences even though they may not originate from direct personal experience. People's implicit associations with members of other social groups can be influenced by a variety of factors, including upbringing, media portrayals, and cultural conditioning.

How Implicit Biases is Calculated

In 1995, social psychologists Mahzarin Banaji and Tony Greenwald first used the term implicit bias. They put forth the theory of implicit social cognition in a seminal paper, suggesting that unconscious associations and judgments shaped social behavior.

To bolster their theory, Banaji and Greenwald released their now-famous Implicit Association Test (IAT) in 1998. The test measures how long it takes a person to choose between two options by displaying a series of words and images to respondents via a computer program.

For example, subjects may be shown pictures of faces from various racial backgrounds along with a positive or negative word. After seeing an image of a person of one race, the subjects were instructed to click on a positive word, and when they saw an image of a person of another race, they were instructed to click on a negative word.

According to the researchers, a faster click indicates a stronger unconscious association in a person. The researchers hypothesize that an implicit negative bias toward members of a particular race would be present if someone consistently clicks on a derogatory word whenever they see a member of that race.

The Implicit Association Test (IAT) has been used to assess implicit biases regarding gender, weight, sexual orientation, disability, and other categories in addition to implicit racial attitudes. Over the past ten years, the IAT has become more widely used and popular, but it has also drawn criticism recently.

Findings suggesting that the test results might not be reliable are one of the main criticisms. It is possible for respondents to score highly on one test of racial bias and poorly on another.

It's also concerning that test results might not always match up with a person's actions. Even if someone has a high IAT score for a particular kind of bias, it's possible that this does not fully reflect how they would interact with people in that social group.

Implicit Bias and Discrimination Are Associated
Though the two ideas are related, it is crucial to realize that racism and implicit bias are not always the same thing. Overt racism refers to deliberate bias against people who belong to a specific racial group and can be caused by both explicit and implicit biases.

Ageism, sexism, homophobia, and ableism are some other forms of discrimination that can be impacted by unconscious biases. Being conscious of the possible effects of implicit social biases allows you to actively participate in the fight against prejudice, discrimination, and social stereotypes.

Resulting From Implicit Bias
It is possible for implicit biases to affect how people act toward members of various social groups. Such bias has been shown by researchers to have consequences in a variety of contexts, such as the workplace, educational institutions, and legal proceedings.

Unspoken Prejudice at School
People who experience implicit bias may internalize negative stereotypes about themselves based on group affiliations, a phenomenon known as stereotype threat. For instance, studies have revealed that young girls frequently absorb implicit beliefs about gender and math prowess.

It has been observed that girls begin to display the unconscious belief that women prefer language to math by the age of nine. The more strongly these implicit beliefs are held, the lower the likelihood is for girls and women to strive for academic success in math. It is also thought that these unspoken prejudices prevent women from pursuing jobs in STEM (science, technology, engineering, and mathematics) sectors.

Implicit bias may have a significant impact on academic achievement and educational access, as studies have also shown that implicit attitudes can affect how teachers react to student behavior.

According to one study, Black boys and children in particular had a higher likelihood of being expelled from school due to behavioral problems. Teachers were more likely to focus on Black students than White students when instructed to look out for problematic behaviors.

Implicit Prejudice at Work
Even though there may be issues with the Implicit Attitude Test itself, these issues do not make implicit bias nonexistent. Or the reality of bias,

prejudice, and discrimination in the real world, as well as its consequences. Prejudices of this kind have very real and potentially disastrous effects.

According to one study, for instance, Black job applicants were half as likely as White applicants with equivalent qualifications to be contacted for interviews when their resumes were sent to employers.

Such prejudice against racial groups is probably the outcome of both conscious and unconscious biases. Subtle implicit biases can still affect how people are chosen for jobs or promoted to higher positions, even in cases where employers make a concerted effort to remove any potential bias in hiring. Although it can be challenging to completely avoid these biases, being conscious of them and making an effort to reduce them can be helpful.

Insidious Prejudice in Medical Environments
Age, race, or health status shouldn't, of course, affect how patients are treated. Nevertheless, unconscious bias can affect the quality of healthcare and have long-term effects that include poor treatment, unfavorable results, and even death.

According to a study that was published in the American Journal of Public Health, for instance, doctors who scored highly on implicit bias surveys had a tendency to dominate discussions with Black patients. As a result, the Black patients felt less confident and trusted in the provider and gave their care a lower rating.

Implicit bias in relation to other ethnic groups and particular medical conditions, such as type 2 diabetes, obesity, mental health issues, and drug use disorders, is still being researched by researchers.

Unspoken Prejudice in Court Environments
Unconscious prejudices can also have unsettling effects on court cases, impacting everything from the first police interaction to the sentencing

phase. According to research, Black defendants face a glaring racial disparity in the treatment they receive during criminal sentencing.

In comparison to White defendants charged with similar crimes, Black defendants are more likely to receive longer and harsher sentences in addition to being less likely to be offered plea deals.

Techniques to Lessen the Effect of Implicit Bias

Although implicit biases influence behavior, you can take steps to lessen your own prejudice. Here are a few strategies for lessening implicit bias's impact:

Put more effort into viewing people as unique individuals: Take the time to think about each person as an individual rather than using stereotypes to categorize them.

Try to intentionally modify your stereotypes: If you are aware that your reaction to someone may be influenced by prejudices or preconceived notions, try to intentionally modify your response.

Spend some time pausing to think: To lessen reflexive responses, consider possible biases and counter them with uplifting instances of the stereotyped group.

Modify your viewpoint: Think about things from another person's point of view. How would you respond if the circumstances were the same for you? What factors might affect someone's conduct in a particular setting or situation?

Boost your exposure by associating with more individuals from diverse racial backgrounds. Explore their culture by going to exhibitions or community events.

To cultivate mindfulness and become more conscious of your thoughts and behaviors, try yoga, meditation, or focused breathing.

Although it is challenging to completely eradicate implicit bias, there are techniques you can use to lessen its effects. Reduce the impact of implicit bias by actively working to overcome your biases, considering other people's perspectives, seeking greater diversity in your life, and increasing your awareness of your own thoughts, to name a few strategies.

Although implicit biases are common in everyday life, they can also be concerning. Even more concerning, your unspoken attitudes might not always coincide with your stated beliefs. Although biases against one's own social group are also common, people are more likely to harbor implicit biases that support their own in-group.

Thankfully, these unconscious prejudices are not unchangeable. It is possible to adopt new attitudes, even unconscious ones, even if you harbor unconscious prejudices against certain groups of people. Although changing one's behavior is a process that may take some time, being conscious of one's own biases is a good place to start.

Chapter 3

Perceiving and Feeling

I find empathy fascinating. In particular, how empathy is defined and perceived by others. It's common to use this as a catch-all for all good things; we assume that "being in someone else's shoes" makes things better, but this isn't quite how it works.
Let's agree on the Oxford English Dictionary definition of empathy despite its many variations:

German word Einfühlung, which means "feeling-into," is where English psychologist Edward Titchener first used the term empathy. In the end, it all comes down to realizing the thoughts and emotions of another individual.

Ideally, once we are able to empathize with someone else, we will be able to use that empathy to better that person. We know how to appropriately respond to their emotions. We are not, however, always guided to take constructive action.

Biasedness is the dark side of empathy. It may force us to take a side. If empathy had a monetary value, bias would be represented by it.
In a study titled "The Science of Empathy," Helen Reiss, an associate professor of psychiatry at Harvard Medical School, claims that medical students' empathy levels decrease with training. Reiss admits that emotional empathy alone is ultimately insufficient.

When there is a lack of emotional empathy due to racial, ethnic, religious, or physical differences, cognitive empathy needs to be involved. While emotional empathy, also known as affective empathy, is the actual act of feeling and sharing another person's emotions, cognitive empathy is the capacity to see things from their point of view.

Because of the way humans have evolved, cognitive empathy is extremely important. In summary, we find it much easier to effectively empathize with and share our emotions with those who are similar to us.

Members of the same tribe are most likely to share emotions with each other, or to exhibit affective empathy.

Even in the course of our daily lives, we constantly witness this tribalism. Being a privileged white middle-class male, I find it very easy to empathize with the suffering of another white person who was raised in Oxford. Far less difficult to empathize with Palestinian refugees, despite the fact that their circumstances are unquestionably much worse. I have always been able to turn off the 9 o'clock news with the same thought, "That's terrible", as I head to the bedroom, thanks to my unconscious bias.

Although we wouldn't survive if our empathy was always "switched on," the consequences of empathetic bias are widespread and sometimes quite dangerous. Right now, racism is tearing apart communities and taking lives in America, the so-called "land of the free." George Floyd's life was most recently taken by a white police officer.

Even though there is never a single problem to blame for a circumstance, I want us to take a step back and consider this problem from an empathic perspective.

I don't think the policeman lacks empathy; I'm sure he has empathy for his own family; it's just that he doesn't have it for people who are different from him. It's no secret that humans are biased toward empathy; we find it easier to sympathize with those who are similar to us. Although empathy is a very valuable skill, it can also be harmful because it can lead us to unintentionally or even intentionally group people together. Without action, this empathy bias will continue to feed into the global hate movement, undermining our capacity to empathize with and care for those who are unlike us. Reiterating Reiss's worries for medical students, cognitive empathy needs to be engaged whenever there is a rift between individuals due to race, ethnicity, culture, or any other factor.

I am not an expert on the subject of police brutality towards ethnic minorities; it is a complicated one. Even though empathy by itself cannot resolve the incredibly complex problems that exist in our world, raising empathy levels will encourage people to take constructive action. Whether that be through speaking out, campaigning, organizing communities around a cause, lobbying the government, or applying pressure on politicians.

Acknowledging our tribal nature and inherent racism is the first step towards creating a society that is more compassionate and understanding. We must acknowledge that each of us lives in a bubble, that bias is ingrained in our DNA, and that empathy is a social construct. It's critical that we don't use this as justification for what we do, but rather as motivation to intentionally alter our behavior.
Real empathy requires us to acknowledge that it's a skill we need to practice.

The development of empathy can take many forms. These are a few:

Put the "I" mentality aside.
It's a common misperception that in order to be empathetic, a person needs to be related to or have gone through a comparable trauma. But empathy shouldn't depend on how close we are to suffering or how likely it is that it will affect us.

It's more about making room for others by putting aside your own needs, viewpoints, and experiences, particularly when it comes to social justice issues that tangentially benefit you. We can see how eschewing self-aggrandizing behavior and doing away with the "othering" of social issues that we believe do not directly affect our lives is the foundation for change when we lead with empathy. It is imperative that we begin to view all injustices as something that we must fight together, not just the predicament of a specific group, even if doing so means tearing down oppressive structures that serve our own interests.

Looking through various profiles
The second tactic is making an effort to interact with a variety of people. I deliberately choose to reach out to people just because they seem or sound different, even though I may not have spoken to them before. For instance, when they come to one of my speeches, they might be seated toward the rear of the auditorium. Alternatively, they might be seated next to me on public transport. These are the individuals that I do not have any social media connections with. Finding people with different backgrounds, cultures, etc. is crucial in this situation. Call it profiling, what I've done has worked for me. And when I meet these people, it's all about getting to know them—their thoughts, feelings, and behaviors. It's important to recognize that their approach is different rather than superior.

Pay close attention and listen intently.
In the end, it comes down to listening, giving, and shutting up. All of us are constantly "busy," but if you take the time to truly listen to someone. You can learn a lot more if you listen to someone for an extended period of time without setting a time limit. It is possible to become an excellent listener, and doing so will improve your perspective and emotional intelligence. A great way to practice is to listen to podcasts, radio shows, and audiobooks. After all, listening is a necessary part of self-education, but it requires conscious effort.

Using the police officer who killed George Floyd as an example again, how much time did he spend listening to people and learning about their stories in the communities he served? Asking them about their day. Learning how to improve their community and what he and his associates could do to assist. I'm assuming that he didn't make an effort to understand the viewpoint of the people he is supposed to defend and not hurt in any way.

Empathy is innate, like a muscle, but it needs to be developed. It will wither if it is not exercised and practiced. We need to make a deliberate effort to develop our empathy skills. The problems covered in this book cannot be resolved by empathy alone; much more work, including significant policy change, is required. But if we work on improving our empathy, we can become more engaged citizens and create action-rooted communities that are stronger and more resilient. That's the kind of world we all aspire to live in, isn't it?

if you put in the necessary time. If you resolve to improve just a little bit at it. Your personal and professional life might just take a turn for the better, and if everyone makes that deliberate decision, perhaps the entire world will as well.

Chapter 4

Challenging Microaggressions

Having conversations with friends, family, and coworkers is crucial to combating racism. As crucial as it is to comprehend the systemic and historical elements that contribute to racism, it is equally critical to address "microaggressions." These are the subtle but commonplace examples of sexism, homophobia, racism, and other forms of discrimination that you encounter every day. It may be an insensitive remark or gesture, or it may be an insult.

We live our lives navigating all of these things. For a lot of us, every day, every hour. Furthermore, there are those of us who may not even be aware that we are engaging in them or even committing them.

To be clear, just because something is "micro" in microaggression doesn't mean it can't have a significant, life-altering effect. They can, which makes it even more important to talk to them when you come across them. Well, if you're able to.

The term "microaggressions" refers to regular, subtle, purposeful, and frequently inadvertent interactions or behaviors that convey prejudice toward historically marginalized groups. People who engage in microaggressions may not even be aware of them, which sets them apart from overt discrimination or macroaggressions.

Microaggressions include remarks about how well an Asian American speaks English that imply the Asian American was not born in this country. Another example is assuming that someone who is black is violent or dangerous. Black men frequently discuss being followed around in stores or having people move aside to grab their wallets or handbags when they board an elevator.

People frequently aren't even aware that they're engaging in those kinds of behaviors. Actually, what would happen if you stopped them and asked, "Why did you just move?" Because they are unaware of how their actions expose their racial prejudices, they wouldn't acknowledge it.

What difference does it make if someone says something racist to me? Ultimately, it is racist when someone says something offensive to you. Furthermore, it doesn't really matter how we define it, if it hurts your feelings, then it hurts your feelings.

However, it's crucial to realize that many times, those who participate in microaggressions won't admit that what they said was homophobic, sexist, or racist. Therefore, labeling them as racist, sexist, or homophobic would put them on the defensive and prevent them from even realizing the impact of their actions.

As fallible human beings, we are all capable of making mistakes and committing microaggressions. And if you engage in microaggressions, it doesn't always mean that you're a bad person; rather, it just means that you should be more conscious of your prejudices and how they affect other people. It is up to us all to make the commitment to work on these issues in order to build a more harmonious society.

Let's imagine that you strike up a discussion about the news. The topic of police, racism, and police brutality then comes up. Perhaps there is a tense moment in the conversation and you feel like a microaggression is about to happen. So, what are your options?

I believe that when having what we would call difficult conversations, there are a lot of factors that people should take into account. Consider first if it would be worthwhile to speak with the person. Is this someone you have feelings for? Is this someone you genuinely believe would be able to listen to what you have to say? People argue frequently with people with whom they don't necessarily need to have an emotional attachment because they don't have that kind of relationship.

It could be crucial to simply state, "Look, I feel like we're both getting really emotionally charged right now," if you are close and in a relationship. It seems as though I am not able to hear you. It doesn't seem like you can hear me when I speak. That means we might want to put this on hold and discuss it later. Alternatively, offer them something to read; that might be more beneficial or efficient than a discussion that could end up degenerating into antagonism and yelling.

People of color are frequently asked to teach white people about issues they have lived with and thought about their entire lives. For someone to then have to worry about the feelings of the white person and put in the extra effort to learn something that they should have and could have learned throughout their life can be extremely draining on a psychological and emotional level.

Don't do that if that's not what you want to do. Alternatively, you could give them some reading material or resources to peruse before they even join the conversation.

However, you might need to complete that homework if you're a person with privileged identities and you want to be a true ally. Perhaps you are forced to experience those uncomfortable feelings because you understand that it is your duty and obligation to have these conversations in order to spare other women, people of color, or LGBTQ people from having to do so on your behalf.

Moreover, there might be some unease if you're discussing a group that isn't present in the discussion. Despite the fact that none of us are black, we are discussing police brutality against Black people here.

It is not necessary to belong to a particular group in order to recognize injustice. Essentially, it comes down to developing empathy for other people. And to simply have a thorough awareness of and understanding of history. Racism against Black people and Indigenous people is ingrained in this country and has never changed.

We depend on our knowledge, awareness of history, and the lived experiences of those groups' members, even though we may not fully comprehend what it means to be a member of the targeted group at that particular time.

Assume for the moment that we are close friends discussing what it means to be brown in New York. I could do better, you know, but we're friends, and then I say something homophobic. What next steps do you take?

'What do you mean by that?' is what I might ask you right away. 'Oh, that's so gay,' someone remarks. 'What do you mean by that?' I ask after that. And if we're friends, it means that I have faith in your commitment to social justice causes and that perhaps this was just an error for which the other person will later apologize. I did not mean to say that. Because you're giving someone the chance to clarify themselves by finding out what they mean when they say that.

Furthermore, some people only say things because they have been socialized to say them. But, when pressed to clarify their remarks, they are forced to consider them carefully and occasionally even backtrack because they don't want to perpetuate an image of themselves that isn't truly who they are.

What are three quick tips that you would give someone who is having these tough conversations?

Before you even arrive, finish your own work. Examine personal essays and blogs, watch documentaries, learn about the lived experiences of historically marginalized groups, and make an effort to think beyond your own perspective.

Be specific about the outcomes you hope to achieve from these discussions. Consider whether this is truly helpful as well. Do I think this is a conversation that will be helpful in any way? Recognizing that no one will pick up everything in a single conversation is crucial.

While having these discussions, keep your own well-being and mental state in mind at all times. If everyone constantly fought for social justice, we would be having fruitful debates and fights, holding daily protests, and changing laws. However, since we are also human and require rest, we are unable to do this.

However, consider your role and positionality once more. If you are a privileged person and you have the ability to fight for a little while longer, then do so. However, in order to carry on this struggle for justice, we want you to live and be healthy if you belong to a historically marginalized group.

Chapter 5

Creating Inclusive Environments

Since they advance equality and diversity, representation and inclusion are crucial. Everyone can share their distinct viewpoints and experiences at the table, resulting in better decisions and a stronger sense of community. Feelings of inequality and exclusion may result from certain groups being excluded or marginalized in the absence of representation and inclusion.

Additionally, inclusion and representation can promote greater empathy and understanding amongst various groups and aid in the removal of barriers. This has the potential to foster a more cohesive community where members support one another and collaborate to achieve shared objectives.

Methods for Ensuring Inclusion and Representation: Make an effort to engage marginalized groups: Actively interacting with underrepresented groups is the first step towards guaranteeing representation and inclusion. This may entail collaborating with neighborhood associations, holding town halls or other gatherings, and distributing questionnaires to get input from various communities.

Establish diverse leadership: It's critical to have leadership that reflects the variety of the community. This implies that leaders ought to have a range of viewpoints, experiences, and backgrounds from various industries. By doing this, it will be ensured that decisions are made in the interests of the community as a whole and that other voices are heard.

Resources and assistance: Another crucial strategy for guaranteeing inclusion and representation is to offer underrepresented groups assistance and resources. This can entail conducting seminars or training sessions, developing mentorship initiatives, and providing resources or funding to small companies or neighborhood associations.

Promote an inclusive culture: It's critical to promote an inclusive culture in the community. This can entail fostering empathy and understanding, celebrating various cultures and customs, and providing opportunities for people to interact and get to know one another.

Advantages of Inclusion and Representation

Improved Decision-Making a community that is inclusive and diverse can represent a wider range of needs and concerns, which can result in better decision-making.

Enhanced Civic Engagement: Individuals are more inclined to actively engage in community life when they perceive that their opinions are valued and that their voices are being heard.

Social Cohesion: We can create a more harmonious and peaceful society where people are more likely to collaborate towards common goals and aspirations by fostering empathy and understanding amongst diverse communities.

More Invested and Engaged Community: An inclusive community makes all of its members feel like they belong, which strengthens the sense of community.

Decreased Risk of Conflict: A community that is inclusive and representative can lessen the likelihood of conflict between various groups, fostering a more tranquil and harmonious community.

Inclusion and representation are crucial for creating a vibrant and strong community. We can guarantee that everyone has a seat at the table by actively seeking to connect with underrepresented groups, developing diverse leadership, offering resources and assistance, and cultivating an inclusive culture. A representative and inclusive community has many advantages, such as improved decision-making, higher levels of civic engagement, and a more robust sense of community.

Chapter 6

Advocacy and Allyship

A straightforward term with unexpected power and repercussions on both a systemic and personal level. The fact that George Floyd's murderer received this verdict in 2021 had distinct and noticeable repercussions across the country, especially among many Black Americans. This word alone suggested a great deal more for a great deal of people, and it could be seen as a referendum against systematic racism and police violence against Black and Brown people.

Sadly, given the numerous criminal court cases in which law enforcement officials are accused of killing BIPOC people, especially Black Americans, a verdict such as this one is comparatively rare. Many people think that this decision is a step toward long-term racial equality and symbolizes a renewed national commitment to protecting all Americans and holding law enforcement officials accountable. Some people think that the verdict won't bring about long-term change and is just the product of a passing trend of attention being paid to racial inequality.

It is not affordable for those who identify as Black or Brown to allow the latter to be the case. After the untimely demises of George Floyd, Breonna Taylor, Ahmaud Arbery, and numerous others, individuals with racial privilege have a chance to consider strengthening their antiracism endeavors in order to maintain both individual and systemic justice initiatives.

In addition to honoring George Floyd, groups have the chance to consider the significance and effect of social justice initiatives during the previous year. These groups comprise but are not restricted to, executives from the numerous companies that pledged verbally to support communities of color in their fight against racial injustice in 2020. Companies must be dependable and dedicated if they want to follow through on their initial promises of racial justice and equity.

The following are some crucial recommendations for reducing feelings of perplexity and incompetence and enabling people to effectively support or advocate for African Americans.

Becoming aware of oneself as an advocate
Giving oneself a characteristic requires introspection and independent thought. To be characterized by a character trait is to be evaluated by someone else on the outside. Too frequently, people who enjoy racial privilege take an outwardly committed stance to promote Black, Indigenous, or People of Color (BIPOC) issues, but they haven't truly had a member of this community characterize them in that way. They might decide to take certain steps or say certain things, but they never give the BIPOC people a sense of support.

Despite the good intentions behind these efforts, they all too easily turn into transient, egotistical, or performative endeavors. They could, at worst, be harmful and divisive. For individuals with racial privilege, it might be more beneficial to find out from the BIPOCs around them what initiatives would help them feel more supported. This strategy is the result of openness, humility, and a sincere desire to bring about real change. This step is the first step towards moving from this moment to a long-term movement.

Regularly consider and accept responsibility
Recognizing and accepting responsibility for one's own biases and blind spots is a crucial, but frequently disregarded, aspect of allyship and racial advocacy for those in positions of power and privilege. This should involve constant contemplation and conversations about the ways in which injustice and privilege can exist both inside and outside of the workplace, even in the absence of a nationally recognized racial event. By humbly acknowledging how systemic racism and individual employees' racialized stress have been disregarded or perpetuated in their organization,

employers can lessen some of the mental load that Black employees carry. This could take place in a number of ways, such as a formal statement to the staff, one-on-one conferences, or a town hall meeting with the entire company. Long-lasting change can be fueled by more open communication and employee engagement, which can result from this kind of action.

The efforts are targeted and pertinent.
The above-mentioned introspection and discussion can spur organizations to rectify previous damaging or painful actions that supported, condoned, or portrayed racism. This should go on since it has the ability to bring about long-lasting change. However, it's crucial to remember that sincere and successful advocacy initiatives involve paying attention to the complaints of people who require assistance and engaging in active listening. This means that instead of shifting the conversation to something more comfortable, organizational leaders would be well to listen to the needs or hurts of Black people. Before addressing other pertinent but less emergent issues like renaming inanimate objects or hiring more Black employees, companies' advocacy efforts should focus on the more pressing racial issues of our time, such as racial profiling, supporting racial justice initiatives, or reducing implicit bias in hiring practices.

Create anti-racism through business
Numerous well-meaning employer actions may have unanticipated negative effects. For instance, the impact is one-dimensional and fails to significantly change company culture when initiatives to promote diversity and inclusion end with satisfying hiring demographic quotas. Long-term, significant change needs to go deeper and further.

The Jim Crow era and America's history of enslaving African people spread the notion that Black people were less valuable, incompetent, and inferior. Making deliberate efforts to ensure that all practices, policies, and procedures challenge these narratives is what it means to integrate antiracism in the workplace. It takes more than just labeling oneself as "non-racist" to prevent the damaging, long-lasting ripple effects of these narratives. Companies ought to actively integrate antiracism into the core of their business year-round, as opposed to limiting their efforts to promote diversity and inclusion to specific periods of the year or during the hiring process. Among the instances are:

- Corporate matching of gifts to groups that support identity-affirming or antiracist causes;

- Policies implemented by the entire organization that hold workers responsible when their behavior violates anti-racism guidelines;

- Mandatory instruction in areas such as privilege, intersectionality, and unconscious bias that advance antiracist activism and culture;

- Continuous access to learning materials that improve staff members' comprehension of current racial concerns;

- All staff members have a duty and accountability to spread knowledge, act to change societal norms, and lessen the educational load placed on Black workers and "diversity hires."

Given the notable stress, exhaustion, and discomfort Black people can feel when asked to teach and inform those around them about racism and race, the last suggestion is extremely important. Dividing the workload equally is one seemingly simple yet effective way to lessen the educational burden at work and the ensuing mental strain on Black employees or "diversity hires." This emphasizes the need for corporate investment in long-lasting, significant antiracism initiatives by stating that all staff members should be held accountable and responsible for educating others and working to change cultural norms.

Encourage Black affirmation in business settings
When the people in their lives affirm that they are significant, capable, and valued, Black Americans and those around them gain. Speaking and acting consistently in line with these statements is necessary for long-term advocacy, even in the face of opposing viewpoints that have been upheld throughout American history. For Black employees, the previously mentioned counter-narratives support a positive sense of their race, which can act as a buffer against stress related to race. Techniques for integrating these stories into an organization's culture include:

Increasing financial investments to support statements of support, such as forming alliances with Black-owned companies or organizing and sponsoring internships for students from historically black colleges and universities:

- Granting employees flexible work arrangements, like working from home, if they reveal that stress related to their race is preventing them from working in specific environments;

- Recognizing significant events and people in American history who uphold the humanity of Black people.

- Actively listening to employees on a regular basis and showing responsiveness will help them feel appreciated and seen.

For the purpose of achieving a degree of racial justice that many Black Americans could only dream of in the past, this moment in history is both precarious and crucial. Organizations can contribute to the transformation of the BIPOC movement from a trendy moment to a transformative one by taking deliberate, modest actions that genuinely make BIPOC individuals feel advocated for.

Chapter 7

Proficiency in Culture

Let's start by admitting that it can be challenging to learn about racism, diversity, and cultural competency. The capacity to comprehend, value, and communicate with members of a culture or belief system that is distinct from one's own is what is meant by cultural competence.

I'm not an authority on advancing social justice, diversity, or inclusion. I'm an apprentice. My goal is to become more conscious and knowledgeable. And I'm picking up a lot of knowledge, such as the need for a broad-based, multifaceted response to foster greater diversity, inclusion, and equity in light of the growing diversity of the American population today and the terrible effects of racism and hate. I'm discovering that understanding hate and injustice is necessary to lessen them.

In America, racism, injustice, and hatred are on the rise. This could be a contentious statement in a nation where so few people identify as racist. When it comes to how we treat people based on their skin color, ethnicity, gender, age, religion, gender identity, or body type, racism creates false hierarchies of advantage and human value. Ibram Kendi claims that a racist endorses racist ideas, acts, or inaction in support of racist policies.

Whether they came here centuries ago or not, immigrants and their descendants have always made up the majority of the population in the United States. Americans are profoundly impacted by racism and the negative consequences of marginalizing others, both as a nation and as individuals. Racism and slavery are deeply ingrained in the national identity of the United States, having been practiced since its founding.

There are significant costs for all of us and future generations, including psychosocial, political, and economic consequences as well as restrictions on our access to opportunities, resources, employment, and education, whether we choose to address these problems or not, whether we actively practice racism or just watch it happen.

It's difficult to break long-held habits and beliefs. Racism is learned and is "a culmination of factors that are deeply woven into the fabric of U.S. society" rather than being inborn. We run the risk of sustaining injustices and causing harm to future generations if we don't change as people, communities, and as a society—either by our deeds or our silence.

How can the pervasive and harmful effects of racism be changed by individuals and communities? I'm learning the following, though I don't have all the answers: It is imperative that racism be addressed at all societal levels. We will never be able to bring about significant systemic change if we always waiting on someone else to solve the problem. In order to create a more just and equitable society, we must both individually and collectively free ourselves and one another from racism. To do this, we must address systemic biases that are pervasive in government, business, education, and other institutions.

Combating racism offers us the chance to fully connect with humanity and treat others the way we want to be treated. Various religious traditions, such as Christianity, Taoism, Confucianism, Islam, Buddhism, Hinduism, and Judaism, support the ethical precept of treating strangers with the same compassion that we would want for ourselves. We can all contribute to the creation of a more compassionate and just world as we seek to lessen racism.

Methods for Developing Cultural Competence
Start at your current position: Tell yourself that it's okay to start learning from here, wherever you are. Starting now, from wherever you are, is preferable to starting later or never at all. And after that, inhale and take a step, then another, and still another.

Acquiring multicultural competence necessitates learning three key skills: recognizing your own cultural biases and values, learning to respect other people's perspectives, and acquiring and applying culturally appropriate interpersonal skills.

Develop your knowledge of diversity and multiculturalism: A developmental process involves testing out old beliefs and picking up new abilities. ***Here are some tactics:***

- Adopt a growth mentality. Be willing to learn about perspectives that diverge from your own.

- Investigate information from multiple sources.

- Make inquiries.

- Have discussions on prejudice, inclusion, systemic racism, anti-racism, and stereotypes.

- Continue to learn, develop, and question your preconceived notions.

Perform the work: As was previously mentioned, performing the work entails reading, learning, and more. In order to do the work, one must examine and become more conscious of oneself, examine and acknowledge their own prejudices, and strive to become more aware of their privilege. This is a continuous process of self-awareness and self-development rather than a one-time event.

Join forces with others: Talk about and take action on issues related to anti-racism, diversity, and inclusion. Assemble or join a conversation group. Attend a course. Engage in conversation with members of other racial, ethnic, or religious groups. Join a task force to bring about constructive change.

Speak with your kids about inclusion and race: Experts say that adults, whether on purpose or by accident, transmit our attitudes toward race to children. Have racial conversations with your child.

Developing multicultural competency and fighting racism are gradual processes that call for methodical changes in both society and the individual. As we take the challenging and important steps toward building a more compassionate and equitable world, the twenty-first century offers us both the opportunity and the mandate to deepen our humanity.

Chapter 8

Educating Kids

Racism is a spectrum phenomenon. It exists between people, in organizations, and throughout society. Children are impacted by discriminatory attitudes and behaviors on all levels. Racism is ingrained in children from an early age, and they are exposed to numerous messages about it.

Children pick up on a lot of things, including what their parents and teachers say, what they see and hear on TV, the appearance of their dolls, and the treatment of other people in their communities and schools. People absorb everything from their social surroundings. Numerous studies have been conducted over many years to examine how children learn racism and how they comprehend race. However, the science is still far from offering a recipe for combating racism. Numerous factors can impact children's comprehensive comprehension of race, and a great deal of research remains to be done in this area.

Among those attempting to close the knowledge gap are psychologists, who investigate the mechanisms and triggers that shape children's conceptions of race as well as strategies for countering any prejudice they may be exposed to at a young age. It won't be simple to eradicate racism, including White supremacist ideology. However, children can be trained to perform better than the generations that came before them. Racism is something that our society teaches us very easily, but we are pliable. Nobody is a racist by birth.

Early childhood racial experiences
When do kids grasp the concept of race? The fact that "race" isn't the rigid construct that it's frequently made out to be contributes to the difficulty of the question. The fact that race has no biological foundation is widely

known. Race is meaningful because we give it meaning—especially in the United States, where a large portion of our history is built around maintaining these "racial differences." We presume that certain physical traits are correlated with unobservable underlying personality traits.

Infants can perceive these physical differences and begin to react to them even before they are fully developed. Babies start to exhibit a preference for people in their own racial groups between the ages of 6 and 12 months, according to international research conducted by psychologists at the University of Toronto. When faced with uncertainty, 7-month-old babies are more likely to follow the gaze of someone who looks like them. And after nine months, they start to associate happy music with faces from their own race and sad music with faces from other racial groups. The researchers hypothesize that these patterns might emerge from a baby's lack of exposure to people of different races and that these implicit associations might open the door for the emergence of additional racial biases in early childhood and later life.

Children are exposed to a constant barrage of messages from their surroundings during their formative years, which influence their opinions and beliefs about other people. These kinds of messages catch on quickly. Children start displaying implicit and overt prejudice against people of different races by the time they are in preschool. According to research by Kristin Shutts, PhD, of the University of Wisconsin—Madison, White children are just as likely as Black children to make friends when they are three years old. Yet by the time they are 4 or 5 years old, White kids are more likely to select other White kids as friends.

There is evidence to suggest that bias may be associated with the social status knowledge that young children have already acquired. Yarrow Dunham, EdD, of Yale University, and colleagues conducted a series of studies and discovered that by the time they were 3 or 4 years old, White American children were more likely to associate Black and Asian faces with anger while categorizing White faces as having more positive emotions. Children of African-American descent did not exhibit the same ingroup preference. This implies that implicit bias isn't present in ingroups. Instead, children are absorbing the social hierarchy of the culture around them at a very young age.

A strong ingroup bias and preference are formed by the time a child is five or six years old. Furthermore, the world around children reinforces those preconceived notions. People may associate particular meanings with different racial groups if they observe, for example, that Black boys are more likely to be sent to the principal's office or that Black children struggle more when reading aloud. Children live in a world where they frequently make assumptions based on what they observe.

Children have a more sophisticated understanding of race and racism by the time they reach middle childhood. Even though they still harbor the prejudices they were taught as young children, older children start to realize that talking about race might be frowned upon. Children appear to really begin grasping the social norms regarding what is and isn't deemed culturally sensitive and what constitutes discrimination between the ages of 9 and 11. In an experiment inspired by the game Guess Who?, he, Kristin Pauker, Ph.D., an associate professor of psychology at the University of Hawai'i Mānoa, and colleagues demonstrated this by having children guess the person in a set of faces that their opponent has selected using yes/no questions. Asking about race early on was a good way to reduce the number of candidates because in this version, about half of the faces were Black and the other half were White. However, the researchers discovered that most 10- and 11-year-olds avoided the topic of race, whereas 8- and 9-year-olds frequently inquired about it.

Children who are older start to see the race question as more than just a means of winning the game. Their primary concern is their perception in relation to cultural sensitivity and social norms. It illustrates the age at which behavioral changes begin. And that implies that now is a crucial moment for parents and educators to consider intervening.

Children pick up on messages about race from a variety of sources as they develop and learn, including news and entertainment, peers and teachers, interactions in the community, and, of course, families. All children—White children included—learn about race through a process called racial-ethnic socialization. According to academics, eliminating racism will require a more deliberate approach to socialization.

Racial-ethnic socialization, however, also plays a vital role in preparing kids for potential racism and discrimination in families of color. In non-White households, racial socialization takes place within an environment of institutionalized oppression and inequality. While proactive, it also aims to protect.

Based on a framework created by Hughes and colleagues, researchers have most frequently examined four facets of racial-ethnic socialization:

<u>Cultural socialization:</u> Racial pride and heritage messages.

<u>Preparing for bias</u>: Talking about discrimination and coping mechanisms

<u>Encouragement of mistrust</u>: Teaching kids to be leery of environments or other racial groups

<u>Egalitarianism</u>: Preserving individual traits over belonging to a racial group and avoiding racial discussions

These four elements are prevalent in family conversations about race between parents and teenagers, according to surveys and interviews conducted with hundreds of parents over a 25-year period.

Among the four categories, Adriana Umaña-Taylor, Ph.D., a professor at the Harvard Graduate School of Education, reviewed 259 studies and found that cultural socialization has been most consistently linked to favorable outcomes. Studies have demonstrated the positive effects of cultural socialization on children from diverse backgrounds, such as Asian American, Latinx, and Black. There is strong evidence that cultural socialization has a positive relationship with both academic performance and mental health.

Anticipating bias can also be beneficial, probably because it arms children with coping mechanisms for potential marginalization experiences. While similar, the encouragement of mistrust has occasionally been connected to juvenile maladjustment. This could be the case despite the fact that both strategies acknowledge the institutionalized racism and discrimination in society, but they don't provide coping mechanisms for the mistrust that is fostered.

While discussing race with their children, families from all racial and ethnic backgrounds use these techniques, some are more likely than others to favor one over the other. White families are most likely to use egalitarianism as a racial-ethnic socialization strategy, which promotes the notion that all people are members of one great, happy race. Conversely, messages of racial pride and heritage are more likely to be mixed with bias preparation in Black families. Additionally, those messages can constructively counterbalance one another. In general, children's psychological and academic outcomes improve when pride messaging and bias preparation are combined. Unwarranted teaching of pride can leave kids unprepared for obstacles in their path. However, dwelling solely on prejudice and discrimination can exacerbate anxiety or melancholy.

Families of color are frequently adept at having candid discussions regarding race. However, research suggests strategies to improve the productiveness of the conversation. Anderson discovered in a paper that better psychosocial outcomes for their adolescents were linked to Black parents' higher levels of racial-ethnic socialization competency. She created the Engaging, Managing, and Bonding through Race (EMBRace) intervention with psychologist Howard C. Stevenson, PhD, a specialist in racial stress and trauma at the University of Pennsylvania, in order to increase competency. In order to help parents address their racial stress and trauma and better approach racial socialization with their children, the five-session intervention combines trauma-focused cognitive behavioral therapy with racial socialization messages. Before they help parents consider what they might say or do differently as parents, they want to speak to parents and help them unpack some of this.

The issue with color blindness

White families, on the other hand, can afford to approach racial discussions from a privileged position within American society. White parents generally don't discuss race with their children at all. They are not required to shield their kids from prejudice and injustice.

When they do bring up race, they usually wait until the children are older to have the discussion. Parents erroneously believe their children aren't prepared. Although research indicates that toddlers can comprehend the concept of race, participants in the study of American adults estimated that children begin to process and comprehend race at the age of five. The researchers discovered that the greatest predictor of postponing conversations about race was the conviction that kids weren't developmentally ready. Before parents bring up the subject, there may be years during which children begin to consider race and form their own opinions about it. Parents are missing out on a chance to contribute to the positive direction of that conversation.

Youngsters are exposed to racism and race issues from an early age; if the topic is avoided or discussed later, they will have to fill in the details on their own. Children witness systemic inequity everywhere they look—in the media, in their communities, and at school. Children witness de facto segregation even in integrated schools. They witness children of the same race attending the same clubs and activities or dining together at lunch. Kids are attaching meaning to race because of all of these factors, and no one is correcting their conclusions. Even if they are informed that everyone has equal opportunities, they will still make their own judgments and give the outward look more significance.

Encouraging a "color-blind" or more egalitarian viewpoint may be detrimental to interracial relationships. Children are less likely to report making friends with kids of different races when their parents instill colorblind attitudes in them. It seems to me that educating children about equality helps them to hold onto their sense of privilege. Children may believe that if race is irrelevant, they would prefer to be with the group with superior results.

People who are color blind may also be less able to detect discrimination. Youngsters who were taught about diversity and values were more likely to identify discrimination when it happened. Furthermore, they were more likely to present their observations in a way that encouraged teachers to step in and help.

Schools are important places for teaching about race and discrimination, even though children learn about race at home from very young ages. It is evident that educational institutions, akin to households, utilize various modalities to communicate ideas. The curriculum selections, policies, practices, and images used in the classroom are just a few instances of how racial-ethnic socialization is facilitated in the educational setting.

Kids rely on instructors to understand how to manage racial conventions and what's proper to say and do. And what instructors don't say is frequently as essential as what they do say. Pauker and Elizabeth Brey, Ph.D., of the University of Hawai'i Mānoa, studied the influence of teachers' nonverbal conduct in a research in which they allocated children aged 5 to 8 to either orange or green groups. Because students already have preexisting beliefs about race, the researchers established these groupings as a surrogate for social categories. After watching how other kids from each group were handled by teachers, children answered questions regarding new students from each group. When asked who was smarter, they identified students who had been in the group and got favorable nonverbal feedback from professors, such as smiles and nods. When children have competing sources of information, they typically rely on nonverbal behavior to supply them with information. They build preconceptions depending on how the instructor is engaging with other pupils.

Yet instructors may surely have good influences as well. When the educational atmosphere is one where diverse cultures and backgrounds are embraced and appreciated, pupils are better adjusted. Umaña-Taylor designed an eight-session, teacher-led intervention called the Identity Project that gives teenagers tools and tactics with which to analyze their racial and ethnic backgrounds while they explore conceptions of their own identity. The intervention was associated with enhanced psychosocial functioning one year later. The intervention fosters good identity development for all kids, including White students and students of color. That has enormous ramifications for their personal adjustment, and for society as a whole, as individuals who have a clearer sense of themselves are more likely to connect with others who are different from them.

The Importance of Teaching

For parents, teachers, and other adults who wish to help children comprehend race and prejudice, awareness is a wonderful start. White parents who are more conscious of racial prejudice are more inclined to discuss race with their children. But awareness is the first little step on a long path.

Hughes leads community seminars to assist parents in learning to talk about race with their children, and she noted that while most attendees are well-intentioned, they're typically worried about how and when to start the topic. Her advice: Just start. The anxiety of talking about race leads parents to avoid talking about it at all. But you can't merely respond to circumstances as they happen or wait for your kids to ask questions. You need to be thoughtful about what you want your kids to know about race. If you can't find exactly the correct words, don't stress. Childhood happens over a long period, and you get to keep rehearsing this discourse.

Meaningful intergroup contact is also necessary for instruction acceptance. Yet it's not enough to merely sit next to a Black man on a bus or converse with a Latinx supermarket clerk. It needs to be meaningful, long-term contact. Being exposed to adults and kids from other origins is one of the finest tools psychology has to give for establishing favorable views toward other groups.

In many areas, that's tough. It might be effortful for parents to find opportunities for youngsters to see individuals who look different than they do. Choosing diverse towns and schools, connecting with babysitters or instructors from various groups, and even pen pal programs that link youngsters from different backgrounds can all be strategies to start breaking down barriers. Parents would also be wise to look closely at their own interactions. If you're telling children you respect variety yet you have little diversity in your friendships, they pick up on that contradicting message.

Teachers, too, should be having talks about race with even very young pupils. But most instructors are White, and there's a need for new tools to help them integrate race and diversity in their courses. Teachers need experience, and they need training in dealing with racial issues in their classrooms.

Efforts are being made to meet that need. The Southern Poverty Law Center's Learning for Justice project (previously Teaching Tolerance) is in its 30th year trying to eradicate hatred by battling intolerance in schools. The project, which provides free tools and assistance to help educators battle against racial injustice and support student and community action, has plans to expand its reach to caregivers and other groups in 2021. Many other researchers are also tackling the topic. Among them is Umaña-Taylor, whose team designed a teacher professional development program, Equipping Educators for Equity through Ethnic-Racial Identity that trains educators to undertake talks about race, ethnicity, and identity with their students.

Professional development programs such as this will be vital to promote fair and just schools where all kids may succeed.

Although it's crucial to start teaching anti-bias messaging as early as possible, it's also valuable for youngsters to realize that racist ideas don't have to be permanent. Just because you or someone you know says something biased doesn't imply you'll be that way forever. A preliminary study shows that understanding bias as something that can change, helps adolescents to stay engaged in socializing across racial lines since it lowers the risks that any mistakes they make would be a stain that stays there forever.

While there's been a recent upswing in parents and educators wishing to confront racism, its doubtful there will ever be a unified curriculum for educating children about race. There's no one-size-fits-all model. A lot of individuals desire to create change, but facts are required regarding what improvements would work for a given group or school. Rushing to implement changes that aren't yet established might wind up doing more harm than good, which is why psychological research is so crucial.

Among the many remaining concerns is how best to assist multiracial youngsters in analyzing their ideas and experiences with race and identity. A review of the research on racial-ethnic socialization in multiracial households indicated most parents do not address multiracial identification with their children. Those discussions certainly aren't being handled enough at school, either.

Even while the study continues, parents must keep up the hard job of recognizing their own prejudices and educating their children to do the same. People frequently have a purpose, but they don't sustain it. The books everyone purchased since George Floyd's murder are now dusty. To develop anti-racist children, parents, caregivers, teachers, and psychologists have to work to keep the endeavor top of mind. It starts with us as adults. We need to be continually probing ourselves and others around us. There's no chance we'll be good caregivers if we haven't first communicated with ourselves.

Chapter 9

Taking Action in Your Community

One of the first steps to reducing racial prejudice is learning to identify and comprehend your own privilege. Racial advantage plays out throughout social, political, economic, and cultural arenas. Checking your privilege and using your privilege to destroy systematic racism are two ways to begin this hard process.

However, race is simply one facet of privilege. Religion, gender, sexuality, ability status, socioeconomic position, language, and citizenship status may all impact your amount of privilege. Using the benefits that you have to collectively empower others demands first being aware of such powers and accepting their consequences.

What messages did you hear as a youngster regarding individuals who are different from you? What was the racial/ethnic composition of your school, religious community, or neighborhood? Why do you think the situation was that way? These encounters develop and perpetuate bias, preconceptions, and prejudice, which can lead to discrimination. Examining our personal prejudices can help us fight to guarantee equality for all.

Another strategy to confront bias and acknowledge privilege is to support the experiences of other people and engage in challenging talks about race and injustice. We cannot be afraid to speak out against injustice and prejudice for fear of making a mistake. Take action by learning about the ways that racism continues to harm our society.

As advocates, we learn about domestic abuse by listening to survivors of domestic violence. Similarly, the greatest approach to comprehending racial injustice is by listening to people of color.

It is a common fallacy that we live in a "post-racial" world where people "don't notice color." Perpetuating a "colorblind" mentality actually adds to racism.

When Dr. Martin Luther King, Jr. stated his desire to live in a colorblind world, he did not imply that we should overlook race. It is hard to remove racism without first acknowledging race. Being "colorblind" overlooks a fundamental element of a person's identity and denies the genuine injustices that many individuals endure as a result of race. We must perceive color in order to work together for fairness and equality.

Let people know that racist statements are not okay. If you are not comfortable or do not feel secure being aggressive, attempt to break down your thought process and ask questions. For example, "That joke doesn't make sense to me, could you clarify it?" Or "You may be kidding, but this is what it implies when you say that kind of stuff." Do not be scared to engage in talks with loved ones, coworkers, and friends. Microaggressions, which might emerge in the form of racial jokes or utterances, propagate and normalize biases and prejudices. Remember that not saying anything or laughing along, suggests that you agree.

Systemic racism means that there are impediments – including income inequality, criminal justice prejudice, and education and housing discrimination that stack the deck against persons of color in the job or at school. For example, the African American Policy Forum (AAPF) stated that in 2014, a 12-year-old girl faced criminal charges, in addition to expulsion from school, for writing "hello" on a locker room wall. Their campaign, #BlackGirlsMatter, addresses the challenges of overpoliced and under-protected Black girls inside the education system. Organizations and institutions must address these concerns and foster a culture of equity.

Know the procedures of firms that you invest in and the charity that you give to. Make an effort to purchase at small, local companies and donate your money back to the people living in the neighborhood. Your state or territory may provide a listing of local, minority-owned companies in your region.

Remember that all types of oppression are interrelated. You cannot fight against one type of injustice and not fight against others. Many survivors of domestic violence also confront racism and other types of injustice. We must acknowledge and support survivors' unique experiences.

Conclusion

You could have friends, relatives, and coworkers with varied degrees of cooperation with racism. If somebody makes a racist comment, it's simpler to ignore it so you don't cause waves. Challenging racist statements needs work; it could make you uncomfortable or perhaps result in confrontation or missed opportunities.

You need to be willing, devoted, and able to dispute harmful statements and engage individuals in enlightening talks about race over the dinner table and during board games or ball sports. If you have children, they are observing how you respond to prejudice.

It benefits people of color and everyone else. Racism affects people of color, but it also reduces the lives and destroys the psyche of its perpetrators. When these circumstances arise, explain you're uncomfortable with what someone said because it seemed racist to you. That individual will determine whether to inquire why. If not, try having a subsequent conversation with that individual and ask if you may explain what you've learned and the background that made his statement inappropriate. Maybe that individual will want to converse more. If not, how far you push depends on your connection.

The purpose isn't to win the argument. It's enough if you came prepared and worked hard to halt complicity with racism. But being quiet is never better.

The most essential thing a white ally can do is fight our battles when there are no people of color present. The problem is that too many individuals pretend to fight against the system, yet do not speak out against prejudice and racism when there are no people of color present.

This suggestion may be used in efforts to comprehend any other group suffering from a history of persecution, such as Latinx people, Spanish or Hispanic people, or indigenous peoples.

To be a better ally, educating yourself is of the highest significance as developing your stamina since this is not just one talk and then it's fixed. This is a long-term endeavor. It requires preparation, just like running a marathon. Educate yourself and then commit to being in it for the long term.